The Irish Tenor Banjo

by Dick Sheridan

47
Selections
Reels/ Jigs/ Slip Jigs/
Hornpipes/ Polkas/ Slides

Multiple Keys
Traditional and Modal

To access audio visit:
www.halleonard.com/mylibrary

Enter Code
4997-2897-6302-6162

ISBN 978-1-57424-404-5
SAN 683-8022

Cover by James Creative Group

Cover Banjo: Early 1920s Orpheum No. 3 17-fret tenor banjo by Rettberg & Lange

Copyright © 2021 CENTERSTREAM Publishing
P.O. Box 17878 - Anaheim Hills, CA 92817

www.centerstream-usa.com | centerstrm@aol.com | 714-779-9390

Picks and Strings

Much is left to individual preferences when it comes to selecting picks and strings. Picks, also called plectrums, are available in a wide variety of colors, shapes and sizes, most configurations being triangular, oval, or something called "cat's tongue." Material can be plastic, nylon, graphite or even bone. Some picks have perforations or a sticky substance for a better grip. A friend who used to play warm-ups for TV shows was so afraid of losing his pick that he ran a string through it and around his wrist so that he wouldn't drop it at an awkward moment.

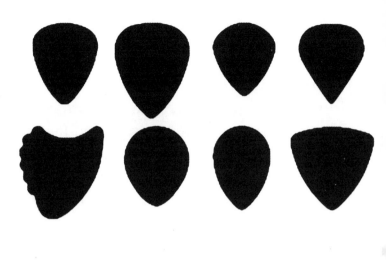

Thickness of the pick is the main concern for most players. Picks are available in a number of thicknesses ranging from light to heavy. Measured in millimeters, a thin pick might be 0.40 mm or lighter, a medium pick about 0.60 mm, and a heavy pick 1.00 mm and up.

Like picks, the choice of strings is also a matter of preference based on gauge and tension. Banjo string thickness is measured in a thousands of an inch. For a tenor banjo in standard CGDA tuning, I prefer a light 1st string (A) with a thickness of .085 or .090. My choice for the other strings in descending order from D to C would be .017, .023 wound, and .030 wound.

Choices for the lower pitched GDAE Irish tuning ranges from .012 to .015 for the high E string, .016 to .018 for the A string, .024 to .028 wound strings for the D, and .036 to .038 wound for the low G.

String material is usually stainless steel or nickel plated. Strings can be either ball ends or loops.

Titles

The imaginative names of Irish tunes is a never-ending source of fascination and often amusement. Take, for example, *Smash The Windows* and *Whiskey Before Breakfast* or the picturesque *Wind That Shakes The Barley* or *Geese In The Bog*. Not to be overlooked is *King Of The Fairies*, *The Hag At The Churn*, *The Lilting Banshee* and *Lark In The Morning*. The list goes on with other tunes in this book and hundreds upon hundreds more in the archives of Irish music.

Drowsy Maggie	The Mountain Road	The Kesh
King of the Fairies	Miss McCloud's Reel	Drowsy Maggie
Cooley's	The Banshee	Donnybrook Fair

Tempo (Speed)

Traditional Irish music covers a wide range of speeds, from slow waltzes to lickety-split barn stormers. Most session music is played fast. But to help the leaning process, tunes in this book are presented at reasonable speeds. Audio files are available for these tunes and can be accessed with an Internet code at the beginning of the book. A feature of these files is that speed can be changed and accelerated to a desired level. Pitch can also be adjusted.

The Tunes

The 47 tunes in this book were carefully selected for melodic interest. They include all styles of rhythms and a diversity of keys, both traditional and modal. These are the popular tunes you might expect to hear at sessions everywhere, universal favorites essential for your basic repertoire.

Typically, most tunes have two sections with each section repeated twice. But there are exceptions. A few tunes expand to three sections, and some have only one. For reference, key names are shown at the beginning of the tune positioned above the key signature.

It is not unusual to find that the same tune can have a variety of names. Some are minor variations, others are totally different. The tune *Glascow Reel*, for example, is also known as *Tam Lin*. Another name for *Miss McCloud's Reel* is *Hop High Ladies*. *The Little Beggarman* is known equally as *Red Haired Boy*.

Bob Lamoy and his 17-fret Gold Tone tenor, model IT-17.

Sources

Many worthwhile tutorials and demonstrations are available on the Internet. In addition is the highly recommended *O'Neill's Music of Ireland*, a standard references work that includes over 1,000 tunes. First published in 1903 and republished in 1976 by Oak Publications, original and facsimile copies are still available. *Fifty Solos For Irish Tenor Banjo*, published in 1986 by the Soodlum Music Co. of Ireland, offers tunes in both standard and traditional tunings. An incomparable online resource is THE SESSION. This outstanding site presents seemingly unlimited tunes in both standard and so-called ABC notation. Each tune comes with a number of variations, sound tracks, comments, alternate names, suggestions of compatible tunes for session playing and links to performing groups playing the tune.

related key signature of D Mixolydian, start by writing the major scale of D: D-E-F#-G-A-B-C#-D. Now lower the 7th tone from C# to C. This gives us the tones of D Mixolydian: D-G-E-F#-A-B-C-D. The key signature is like the major key of G (one sharp).

To determine the tones of different major scales, see the chart located at the back of the book.

For a detailed look at scales see Centerstream's book *CHORD BINGO.*

Techniques

Use of the "triplet" is perhaps the most identifying sound of Irish playing. It compresses three eighth notes into the time span of one and is played with a rapid down-up-down pick motion. Written music is marked with a number 3 above or below the group. An alternate timing is an eighth note linked to two sixteenths or two sixteenths linked to an eighth. A less common triplet variation starts with up-picking in the sequence up-down-up.

Occasionally encountered – although less often than in Bluegrass – are hammer-ons, pull-offs, and slides.

"Cross picking" is a continuous up-and-down picking of eighth notes on the same string or going from one string to another. Keeping the picking hand free of bracing – resting the hand on the banjo head – facilitates speed.

You may have noticed that most tunes are in the favored keys of D and G and rarely call for the 1st fret. Less common too are the 3rd and 6th frets. Shifting the hand up into the "second position" where the first finger plays the 2nd fret and the other fingers follow suite avoids unnecessary stretches, especially to the 7th fret of the high E string.

Sessions and Sets

The gathering of musicians playing Irish music is referred to as a "session." The mix of instruments is eclectic but typically is drawn from the tenor banjo, fiddle, guitar, flute, concertina/accordion, tin whistle, bouzouki, mandolin, uilleann pipes, or the hand-held drum called a bodhran (pronounced "bow-ron.") Search out a local sessions group in your area, or if none is available consider forming your own.

David Deacon plays his unique "Muse Head" Irish tenor banjo.

Tunes are often grouped into "sets" consisting of three or four numbers. The choice is arbitrary, and vary from session to session. Here are some samples dawn from tunes in this book:

referred to as an Irish banjo. Both styles, however, are popular with Irish players, the 17-fret banjo making the reach to upper frets less of a stretch, particularly the oft played 7th fret of the E string.

The Irish style of playing that is current today is one of single notes, not chordal – except for accompaniment – with high speed that rivals even the most accelerated performance of Bluegrass.

The uniqueness of Irish playing is not only the repertoire but the manner in which it is played. Let's take a look at what makes Irish music Irish.

Modes and Scales

Music draws its notes from scales, the do-re-mi's of tones that climb and descend like the steps of a ladder. Most of us are familiar with the **Major** scale. If you start with a C on the keyboard and climb up to the C above it playing only the white notes, you've played a major scale, the scale of C:

$$C\text{-}D\text{-}E\text{-}F\text{-}G\text{-}A\text{-}B\text{-}C$$

For the technically minded these notes are arranged in a series of whole steps and half steps in the order 2½-3½ steps. Irish music uses this scale but with the addition of several variations called **Modes**. A mode is just another name for a scale. An alternate name for the major scale is the Ionian mode. In addition to this mode there are two other popular modes in Irish music, the Dorian and the Mixolydian.

To determine the steps of these modes, first write out the major scale then alter its steps according to the following rules. Tunes take their tones from the mode in which they're played.

The **Dorian** mode starts like a major scale but flats (or lowers) the 3rd and 7th tones. Following the 2½-3½ step order of the major scale of D we see the tones are D-E-F#-G-A-B-C#-D. To make this a Dorian scale we lower the 3rd and 7th tone giving us D-E-F-G-A-B-C-D. Try this on the keyboard going from D to the D an octave above using only the white notes.

D Dorian shares the key signature for C which like D Dorian has no sharps or flats.

The mode of E Dorian, for example, flats the 3rd and 7th tones of the E major scale: E-F#-G-A-B-C#-D-E. Two sharps is also the key signature of D major.

Another example is A Dorian. Write out the major scale of A: A-B-C#-D-E-F#-G#-A. Now flat the 3rd and 7th tones which gives us A-B-C-D-E-F#-G-A. Its key signature is like the major key of G (one sharp).

The **Mixolydian** mode lowers only the 7th tone of the major scale. To find the tones and

A Word from the Author

With ancestral roots in County Cavan and having played the tenor banjo for over sixty years, I feel somewhat qualified to share this collection of classic tunes for the Irish tenor banjo. Who could not love these beautiful Celtic melodies or not aspire to play them for yourself? Never has there been a richer treasury of tunes to sample, some new and some dating back centuries to ancient times before the banjo was even heard of.

They say that the banjo was introduced to Ireland in the mid-1800s when touring minstrel groups first appeared in the Emerald Isle. Banjos were essential to these bands, although the instruments were not the 4-string kind we associate with today's music. They were of the 5-string variety, played finger style instead of using plectrums. Perhaps it was the influence of mandolins that preceded the banjo that led to playing with picks. The history is uncertain, but somewhere along the line the 5th string was removed, the banjo tuned in 5th like a fiddle, and tunes previously relegated to the fiddle, flute and tin whistle were adopted by the 4-string banjo.

Author Dick Sheridan, circa 1960s, and his first tenor banjo, a Lyric made by the Bacon Banjo Co. of Groton, CT.

The popularity of the tenor banjo gained momentum in the early 1900s, primarily as a dance band instrument (easily played by violin players) and in the evolving of jazz from the fading days of ragtime. The new recording industry sent records across the globe, and surely the powerful sound of the banjo would have reached Ireland and attracted players to adopt the instrument to their own brand of music.

The tenor banjo as we know it today has four strings tuned in musical intervals of fifths, each string spaced five notes apart from its adjacent string. The standard tuning, going from low to high, is CGDA. The Irish tuning is like a mandolin or fiddle tuned GDAE but eight notes (an octave) lower. The so-called Chicago tuning DGBE is less common but popular with guitar players since it is the same as the top four strings of the guitar.

Deering 17-fret Artisan Special Goodtime tenor banjo

The tenor banjo is the shortest of the banjo family. Longer is the 5-string instrument and the 4-string plectrum, both typically having 21 frets. Frets are the thin metal wires marking the divisions of the fingerboard. The standard number of frets for the tenor banjo is 19, although there is a shorter variety of tenor banjo with 17 frets often

List of Tunes and Their Types

List of Tunes

Contents

The Last Word

For the new player of Irish Tenor Banjo music, this book provides a valuable introduction. The experienced player will find insights too, a consolidation of information for handy referral. The collection of tunes has been thoughtfully selected for variety, melodic interest, and appropriate chordal accompaniment. Traditional keys have been chosen although sometimes changed for ease of playing.

Tenor banjo players from other styles – Dixieland, folk, sing-along – will find Irish music a new avenue of unending interest. It's an easy switch from standard to Irish tuning, but even without changing the tuning, tunes in this collection can be played using either standard notes or tablature. Simply placing a capo on the 7th fret puts you into Irish tuning with no need of re-tuning the instrument.

Dick Sheridan with his current tenor banjo, a 1927 Bacon & Dey, Silver Bell No. 1

The unique world of Irish Tenor Banjo playing is now ready to explore in the following pages. Much fun and enjoyment is in store for you with this exciting musical experience. Let your mind run free with the imagery of Ireland and the sound of its treasured tunes. With thoughts of a fragrant peat fire burning in the hearth, a gentle mist rolling in off the ocean, and the distant trill of ancient Irish airs, the music of the Emerald Isle awaits you, none of it more hauntingly expressed than that played on the Irish Tenor Banjo. *Sláinte.*

For other fine tunes in the Celtic tradition see Centerstream's *CETIC MUSIC FOR THE TENOR BANJO (CGDA tuning)* and *FIDDLE TUNES FOR THE MANDOLIN (GDAE tuning).* See also *IRISH TUNES FOR UKULELE.*

Tune Types and Time Signatures

REELS	4/4 time
JIGS	6/8 time
SLIP JIGS	9/8 time
HORNPIPES	4/4 time, occasionally 2/4 time
SLIDES	12/8 time
POLKAS	2/4 time

Tenor Banjo Chord and Note Conversion

STANDARD TUNING - CGDA	IRISH TUNING - GDAE
C	G
D	A
E	B
F	C
G	D
A	E
B	F

A Fig for a Kiss

Irish Tenor Banjo: GDAE

Traditional Slip Jig

15

The Bag of Spuds

Irish Tenor Banjo: GDAE

Traditional Reel

The Banshee

Irish Tenor Banjo: GDAE

Traditional Reel

Banish Misfortune

Irish Tenor Banjo: GDAE

Traditional Jig

Banish Misfortune

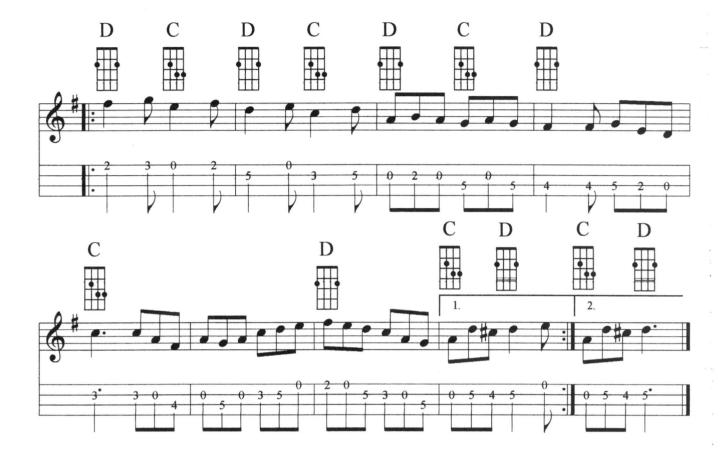

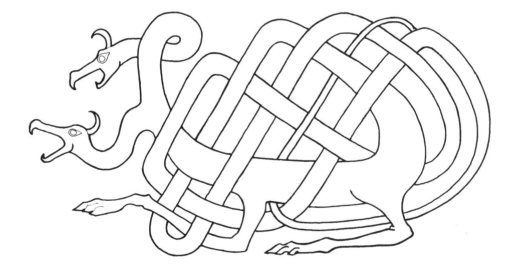

19

Bantry Bay

Irish Tenor Banjo: GDAE

Traditional Hornpipe

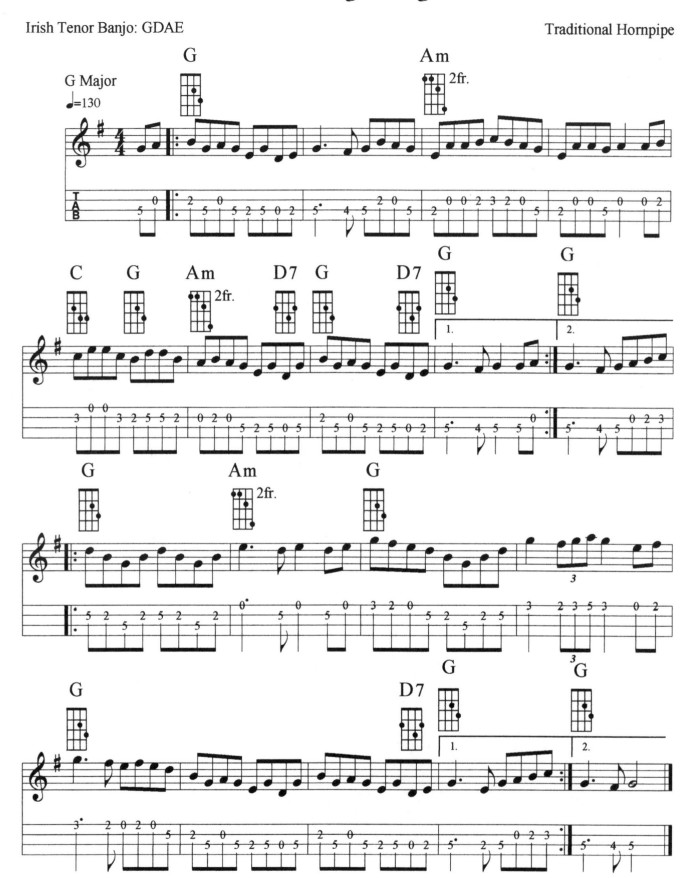

The Blackthorn Stick

Irish Tenor Banjo: GDAE

Traditional Jig

The Boys of Bluehill

Irish Tenor Banjo: GDAE

Traditional Hornpipe

C Major
♩=120

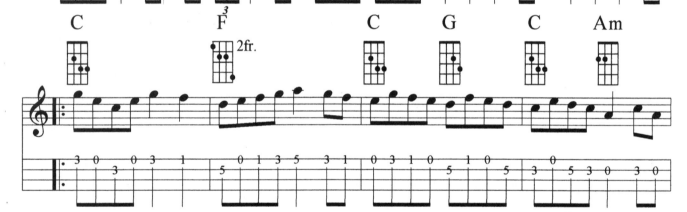

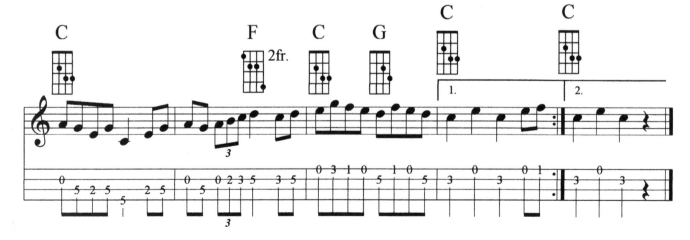

The Butterfly

Irish Tenor Banjo: GDAE

Traditional Slip Jig

Cherish the Ladies

Irish Tenor Banjo: GDAE

Traditional

24

Connaughtman's Rambles

Irish Tenor Banjo: GDAE

Traditional Jig

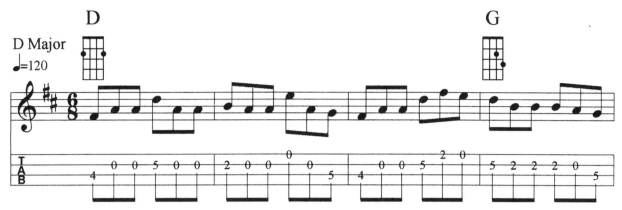

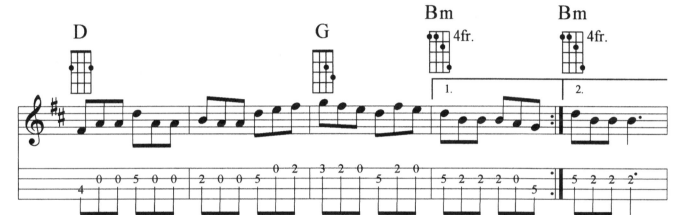

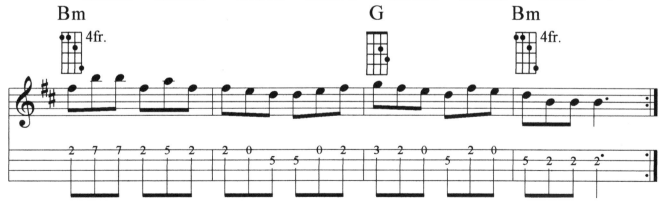

25

Cooley's

Irish Tenor Banjo: GDAE

Traditional Reel

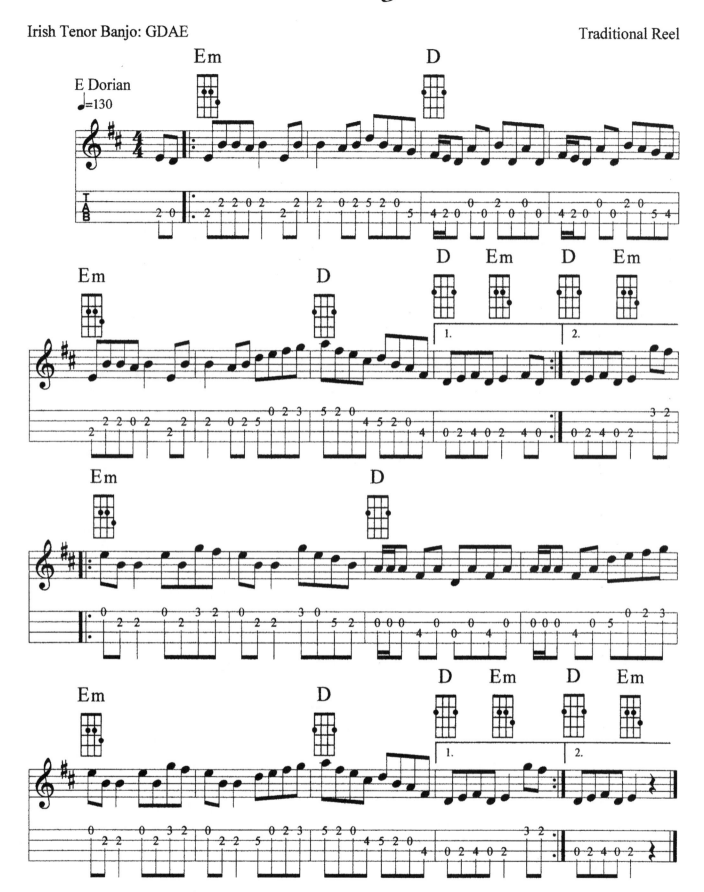

Drowsy Maggie

Irish Tenor Banjo: GDAE

Traditional Reel

Donnybrook Fair

Irish Tenor Banjo: GDAE

Traditional Jig

28

Donnybrook Fair

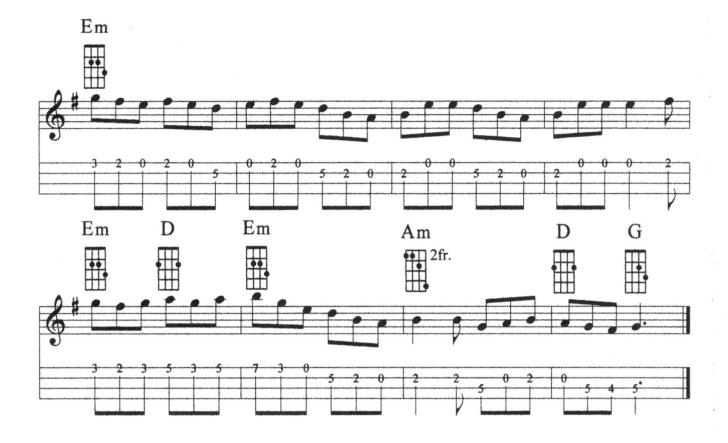

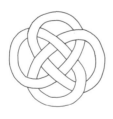

*May you have warm words on a cold evening,
a full moon on a dark night, and the road
downhill all the way to your door.*

--Irish Blessing

Durang's Hornpipe

Irish Tenor Banjo: GDAE

Traditional Hornpipe

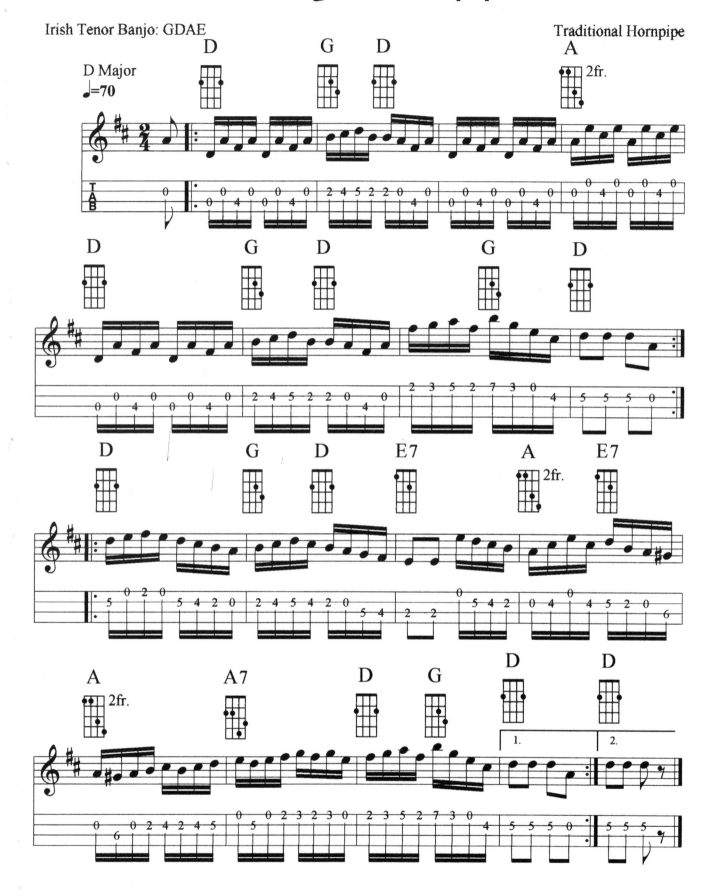

Farewell to Whiskey

Irish Tenor Banjo: GDAE

Traditional Polka

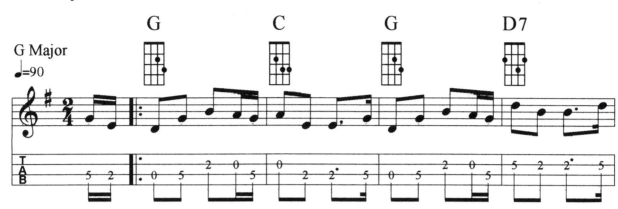

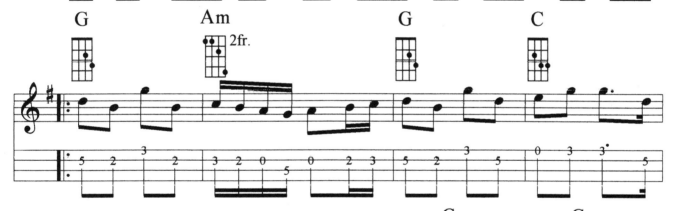

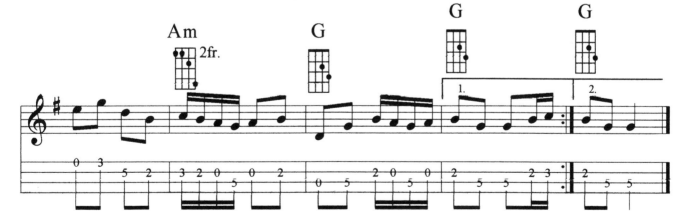

Fisher's Hornpipe

Irish Tenor Banjo: GDAE

Traditional Hornpipe

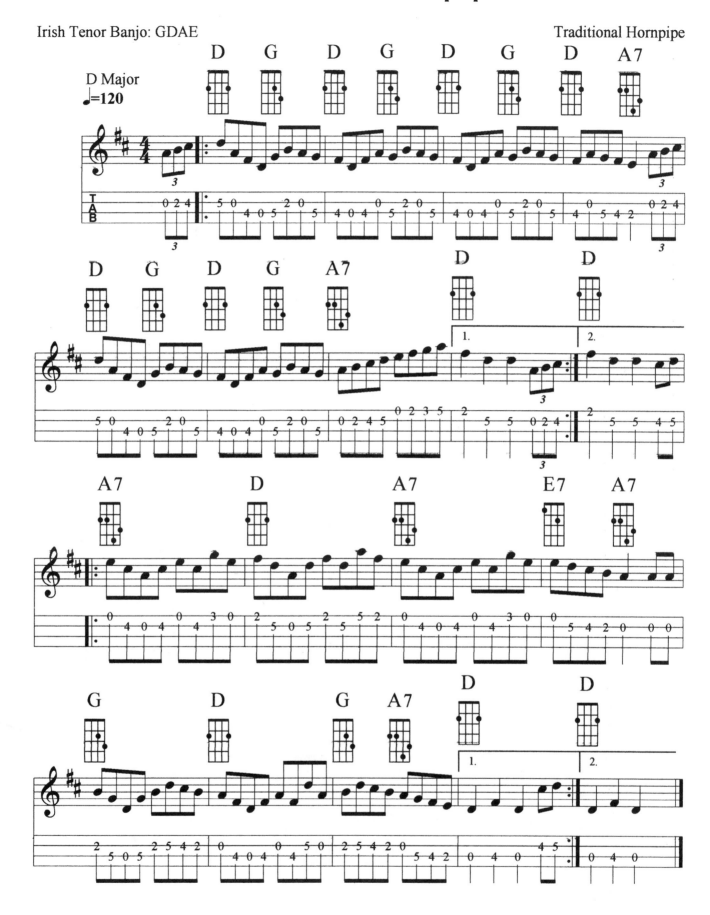

The Geese in the Bog

Irish Tenor Banjo: GDAE

Traditional Jig

33

The Glascow Reel

Irish Tenor Banjo: GDAE

Tam Lin

Traditional Reel

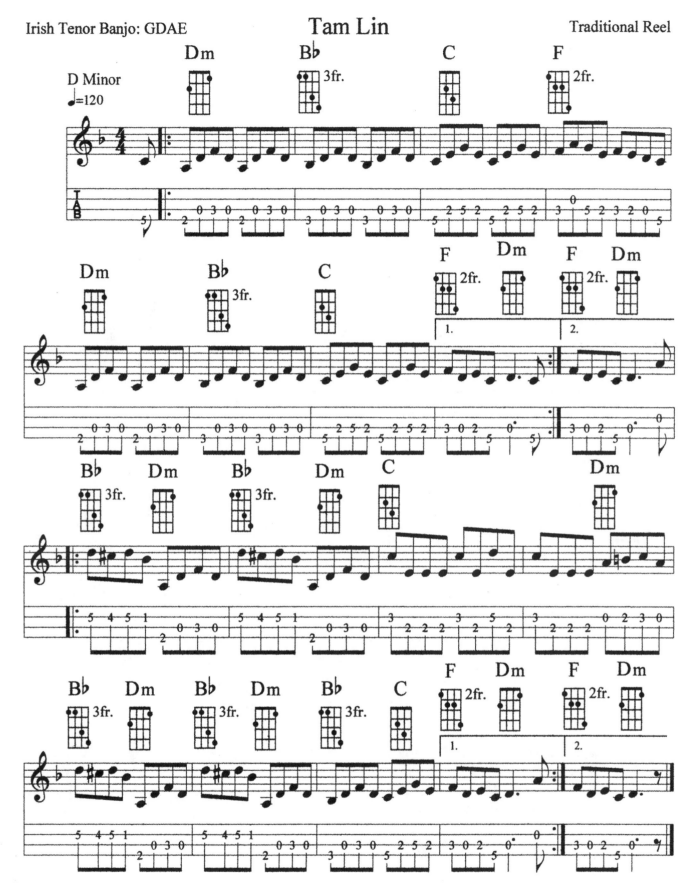

The Hag at the Churn

Irish Tenor Banjo: GDAE

Traditional Jig

D Mixolydian

♩=120

Harvest Home

Irish Tenor Banjo: GDAE

Traditional Hornpipe

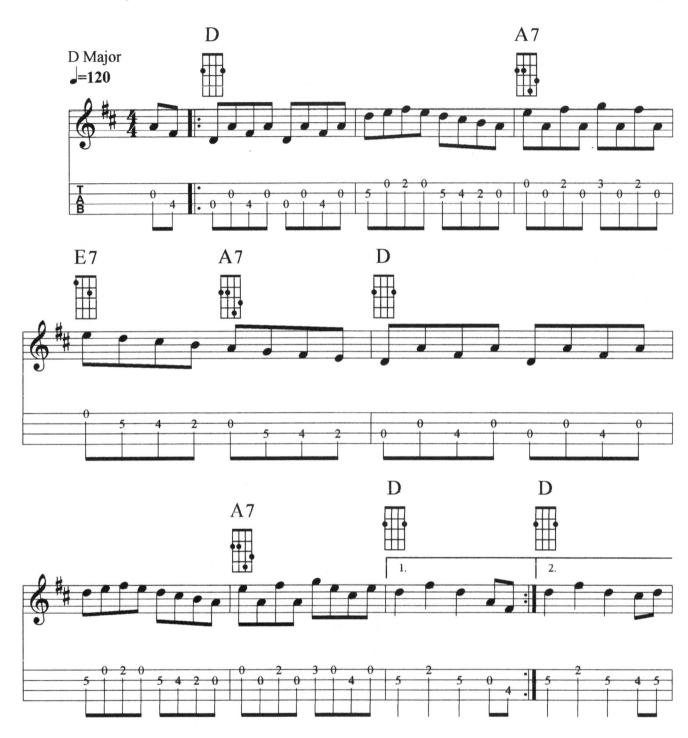

Harvest Home

Irish Washerwoman

Irish Tenor Banjo: GDAE

Traditional Jig

The Kesh

Irish Tenor Banjo: GDAE

Traditional Jig

Kildfare Fancy

Irish Tenor Banjo: GDAE

Traditional Hornpipe

D Major
♩=120 With a lilt

The Lilting Banshee

Irish Tenor Banjo: GDAE

Traditional Jig

King of the Faries

Irish Tenor Banjo: GDAE

Traditional Hornpipe

King of the Faries

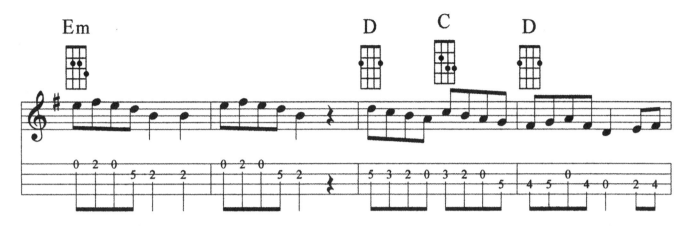

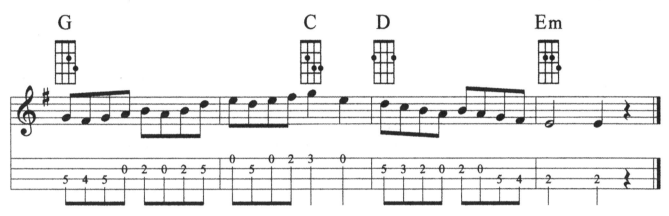

Lark in the Morning

Irish Tenor Banjo: GDAE

Traditional Jig

Lark in the Morning

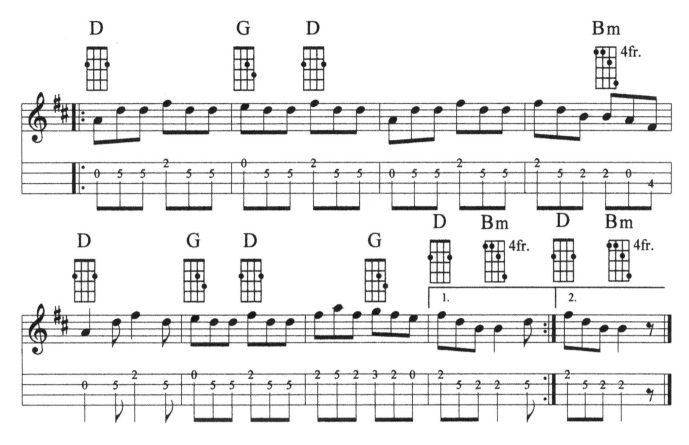

The Little Beggarman
Red Haired Boy

Irish Tenor Banjo: GDAE

Traditional Reel

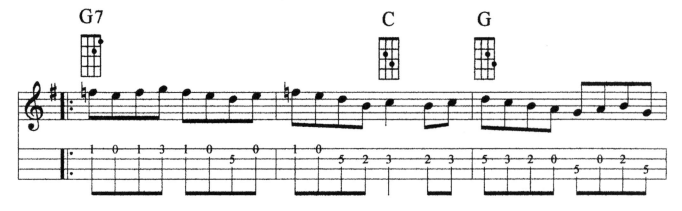

The Little Beggarman

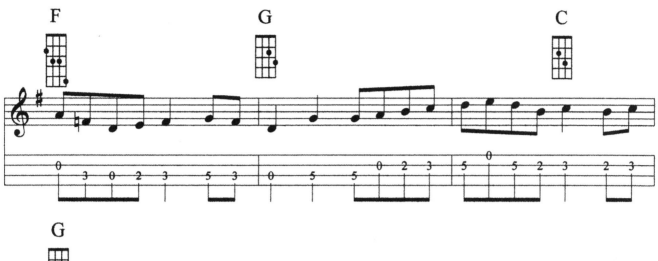

47

Maggie in the Woods

Irish Tenor Banjo: GDAE

Traditional Polka

The Maid Behind the Bar

Irish Tenor Banjo: GDAE

Traditional Reel

Merrily Kissed the Quaker

Irish Tenor Banjo: GDAE

Traditional Slide

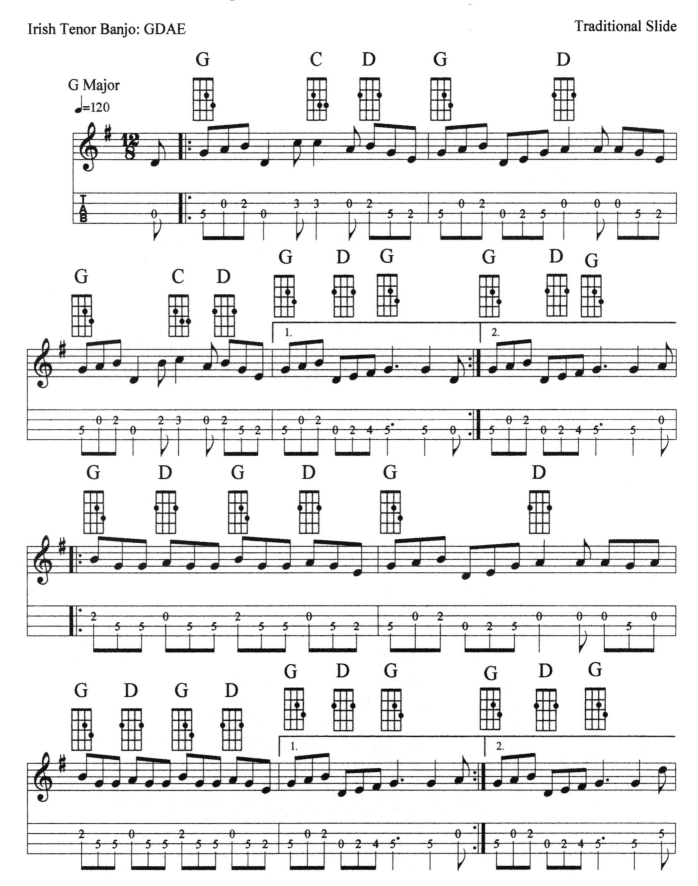

Merrily Kissed the Quaker

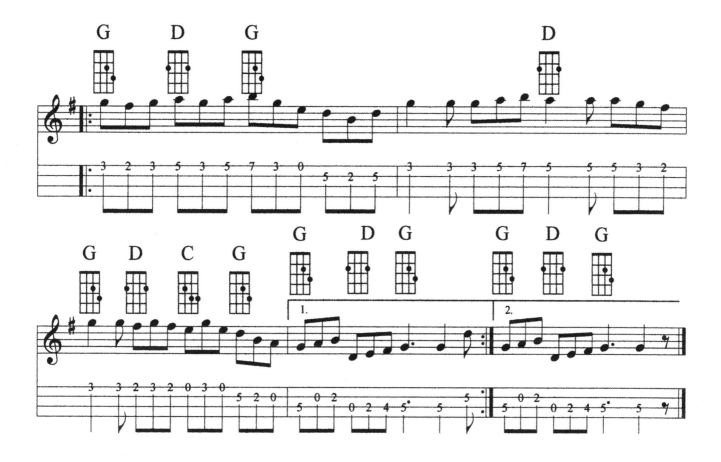

The Mason's Apron

Irish Tenor Banjo

Traditional Reel

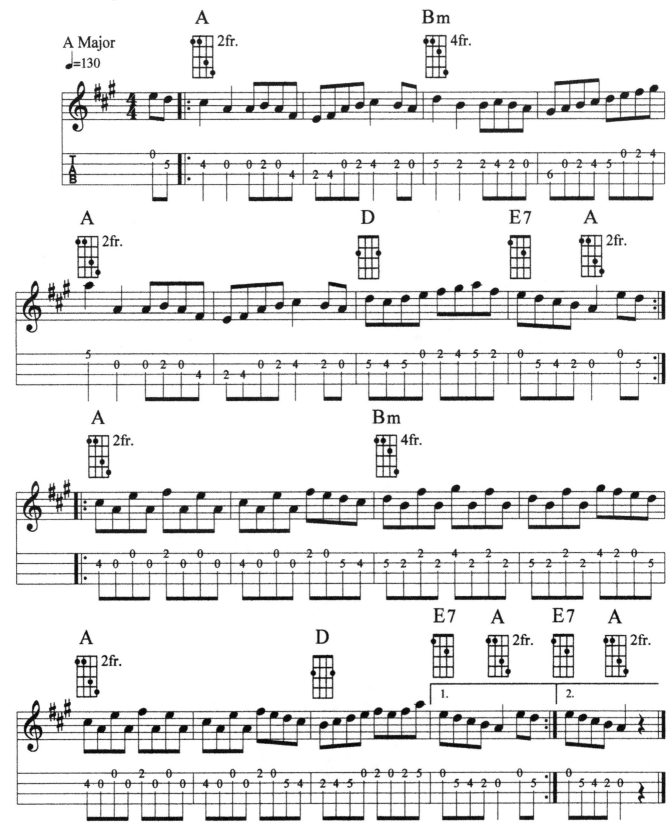

Miss McCloud's Reel

Irish Tenor Banjo: GDAE

Traditional Reel

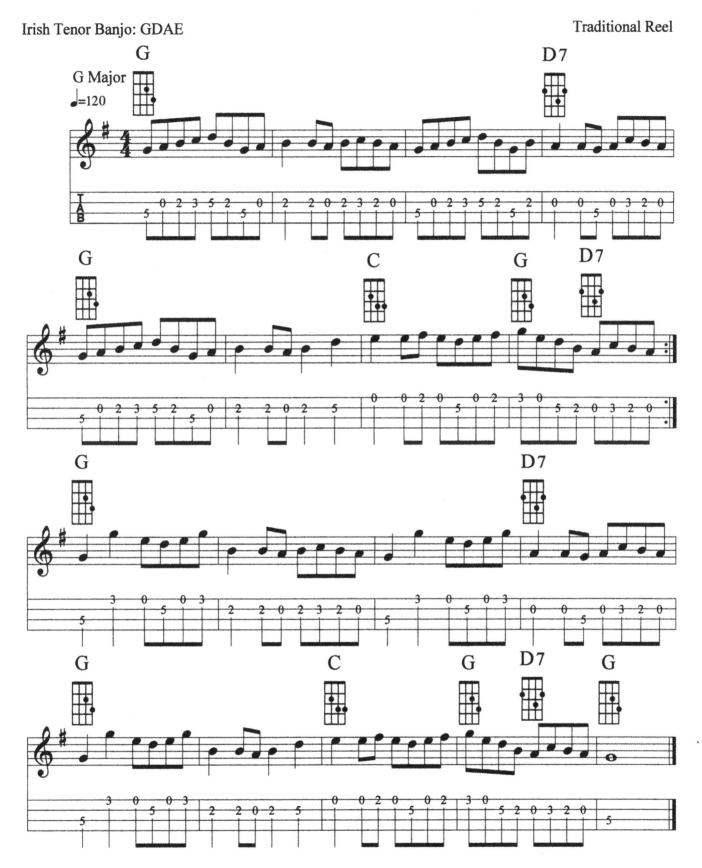

Morrison's Jig

Irish Tenor Banjo: GDAE

Traditional Jig

Morrison's Jig

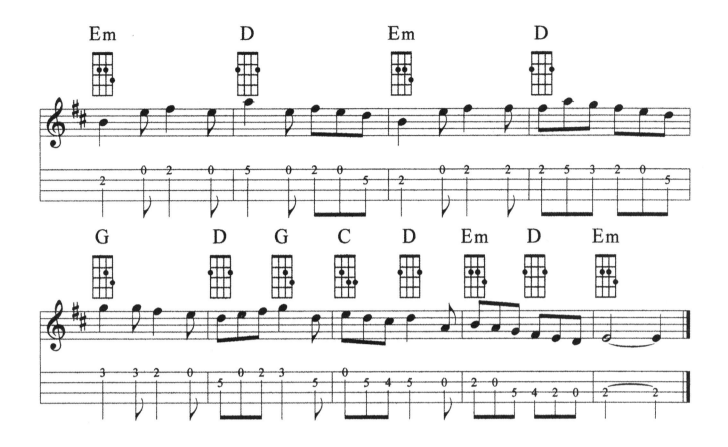

Orpheum No. 3 17-fret tenor banjo
by Rettberg & Lange

The Mountain Road

Irish Tenor Banjo: GDAE

Traditional Reel

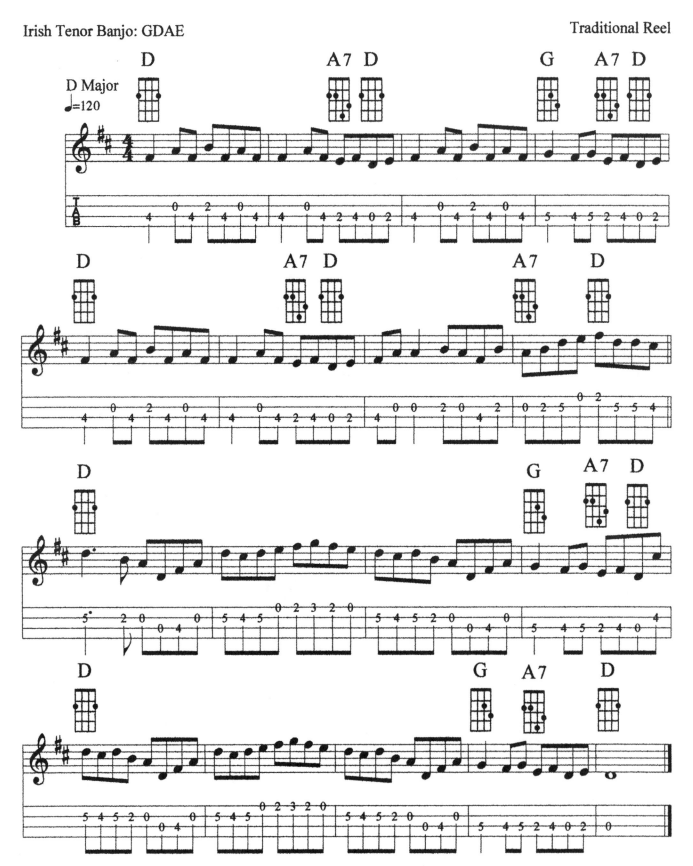

Out to the Ocean

Irish Tenor Banjo: GDAE

Traditional Jig

The Musical Priest

Irish Tenor Banjo: GDAE

Traditional Reel

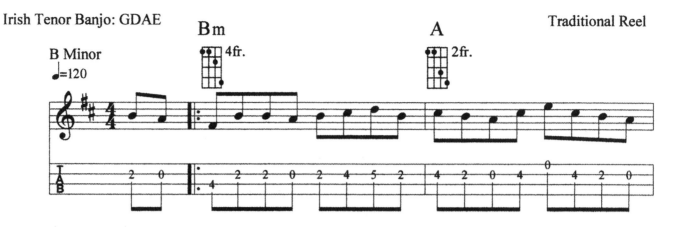

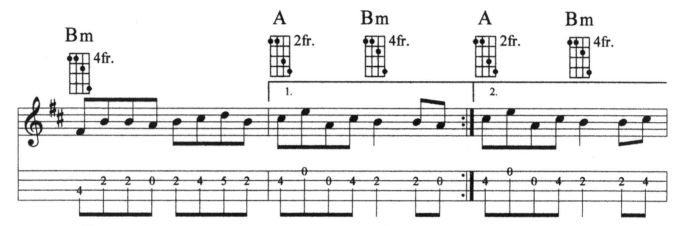

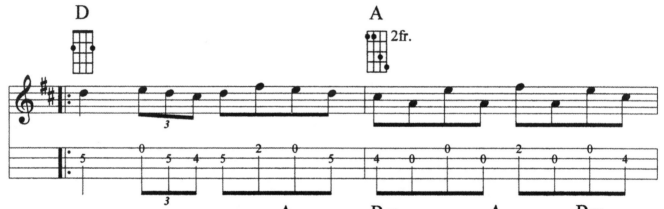

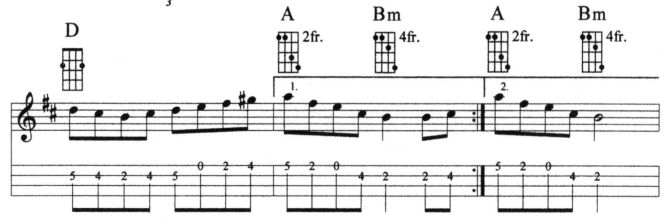

The Musical Priest

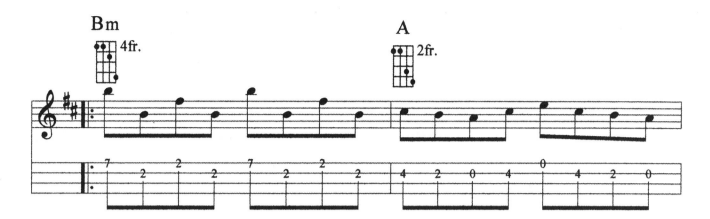

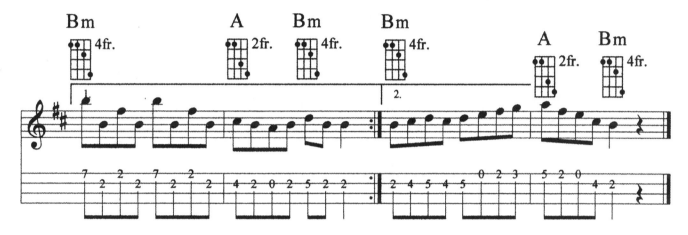

59

Planxty Irwin

Irish Tenor Banjo: GDAE

Traditional Jig

The Rakes of Mallow

Irish Tenor Banjo: GDAE

Traditional Polka

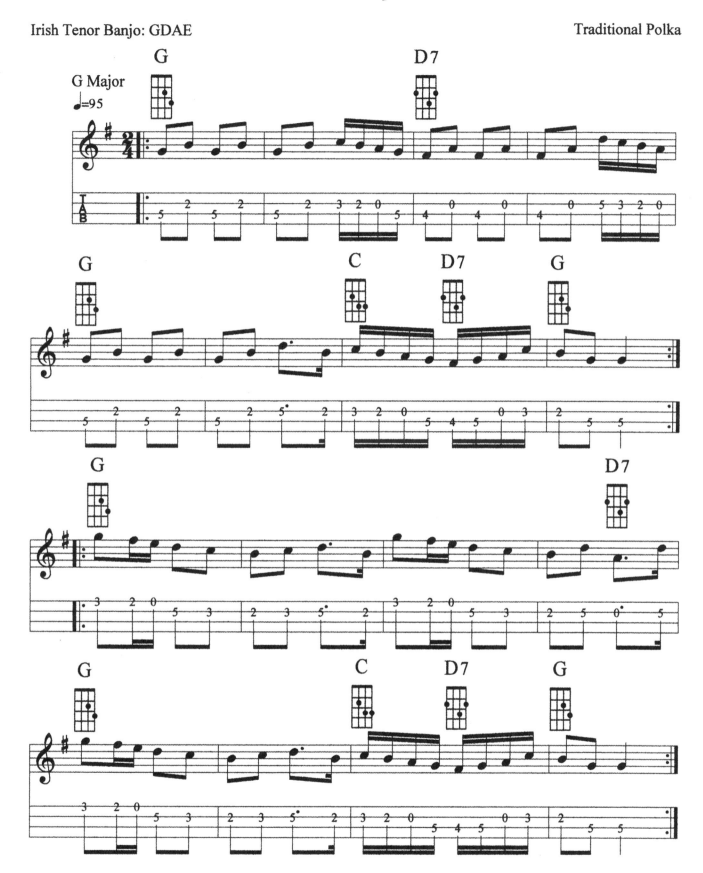

The Rocky Road to Dublin

Irish Tenor Banjo: GDAE

Traditional Slip Jig

62

The Rocky Road to Dublin

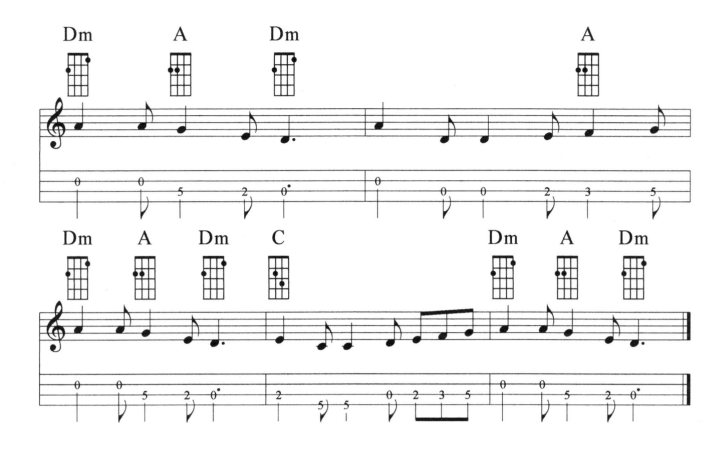

The Road to Lisdoonvarna

Irish Tenor Banjo: GDAE

Traditional Slide

Sailor's Hornpipe

Jack's The Lad

Irish Tenor Banjo: DGAE

Traditional Hornpipe

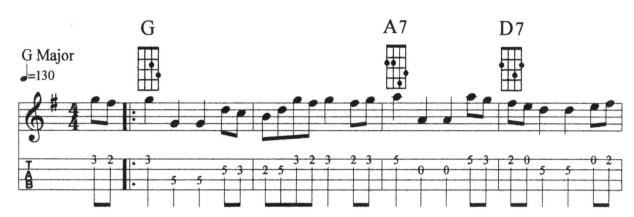

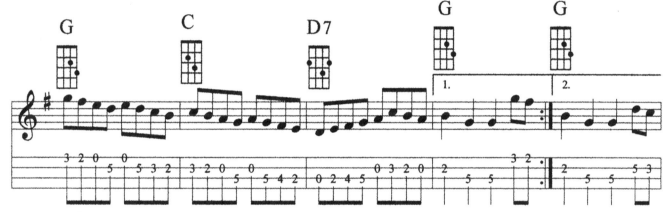

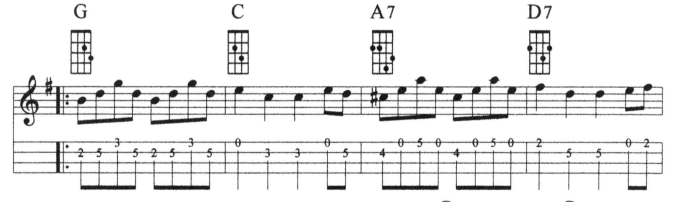

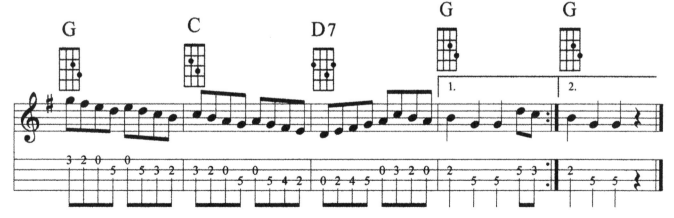

The Hornpipe

One of the most popular styles of Irish music is the hornpipe. Its name comes from an early instrument used to accompany English dances dating back to the 16th century and from which the name of the dance comes from.

Various English composers have written hornpipes perhaps the earliest being a keyboard work by Hugh Ashton circa 1525 simply entitled *Hornepype*. A collection of Lancashire hornpipes is also known from 1705.

The original hornpipe was similar to the *pibgorn*, an obsolete wind instrument made from the shinbone of a sheep with a cow's horn for a bell, the forerunner of today's reeded clarinet.

As a dance, the hornpipe is often associated with sailors doing a stationery solo performance with folded arms and intricate footwork in a lively 4/4 tempo. The hands are brought up to the forehead, first one then the other, in a posture resembling looking out to sea. Similarly, trousers are given a tug, front and back, and many nautical motions – hauling ropes, climbing rigging, and saluting – are parodied.

The tune *Sailor's Hornpipe* goes back to the late 1700s and is well familiar to watchers of animated cartoons as the opening theme for POPEYE.

The Silver Spear

Irish Tenor Banjo: GDAE

Traditional Reel

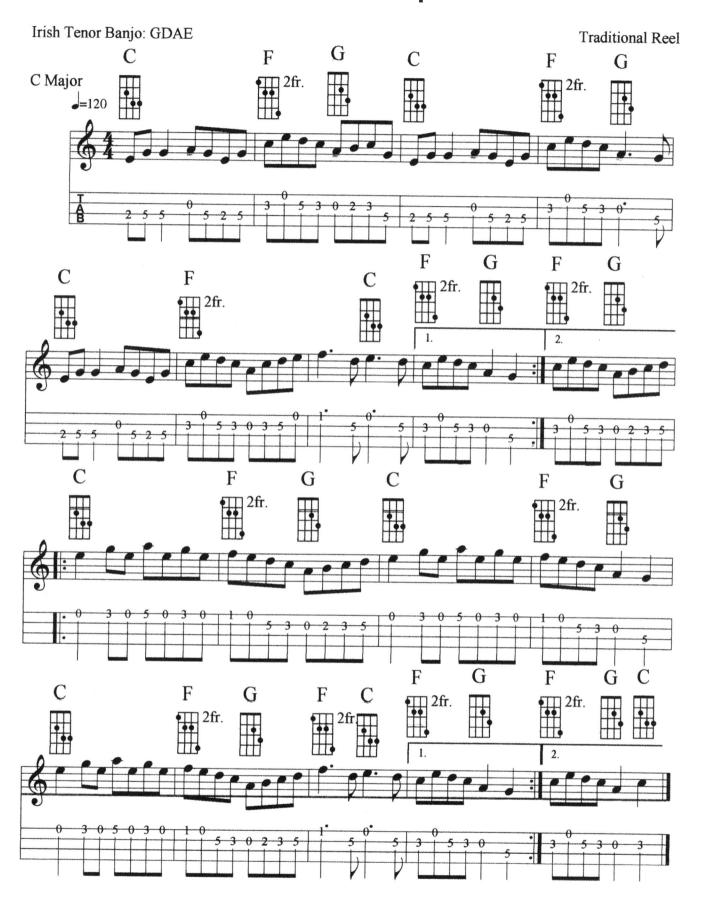

Smash the Windows

Irish Tenor Banjo: GDAE

Traditional Jig

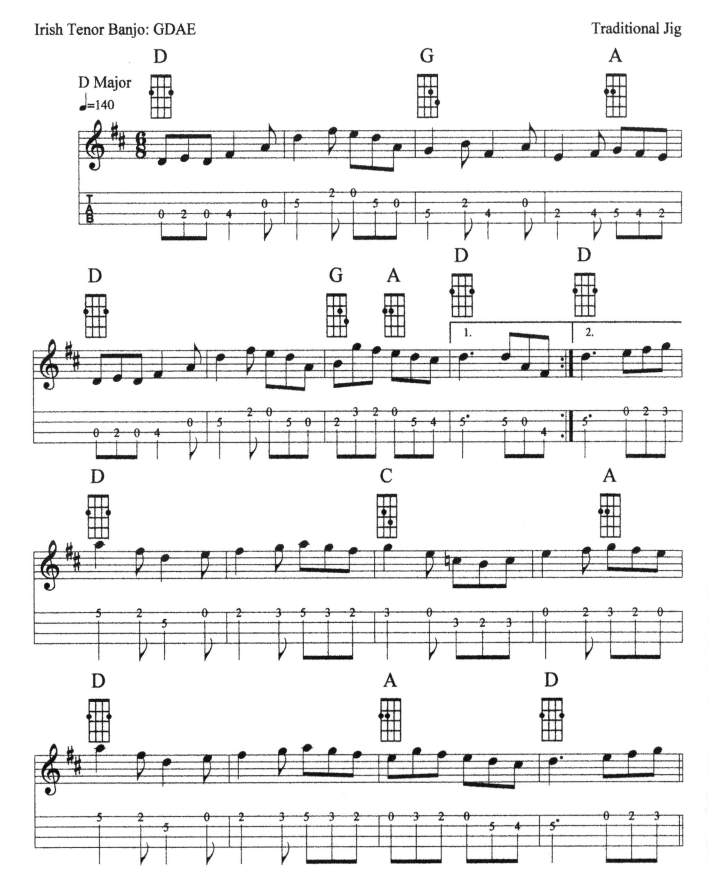

Smash the Windows

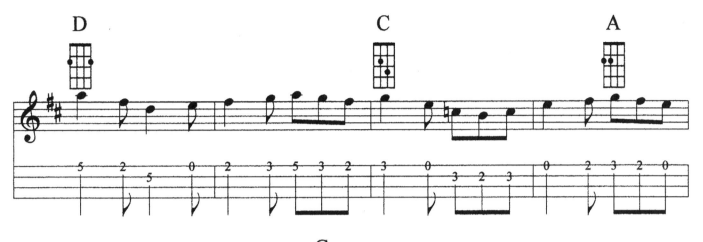

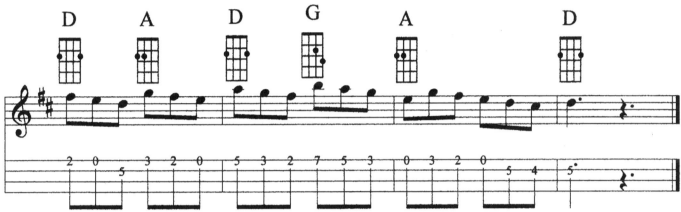

The Tempest

Irish Tenor Banjo: GDAE

Traditional Jig

The Tempest

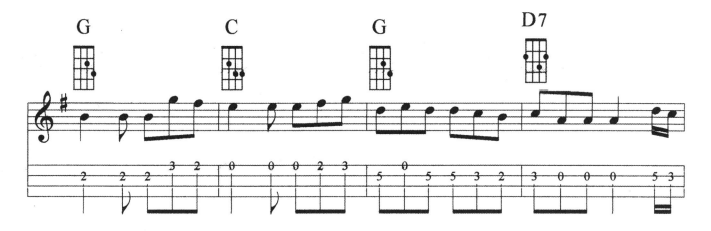

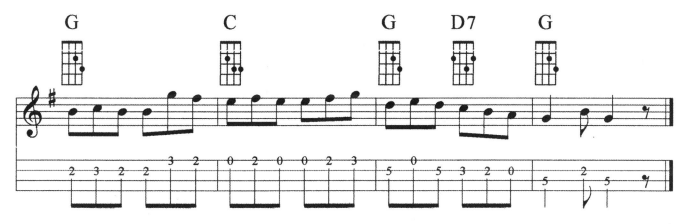

The Swallowtail

Irish Tenor Banjo: GDAE

Traditional Jig

Whiskey before Breakfast

Irish Tenor Banjo: GDAE

Traditional Reel

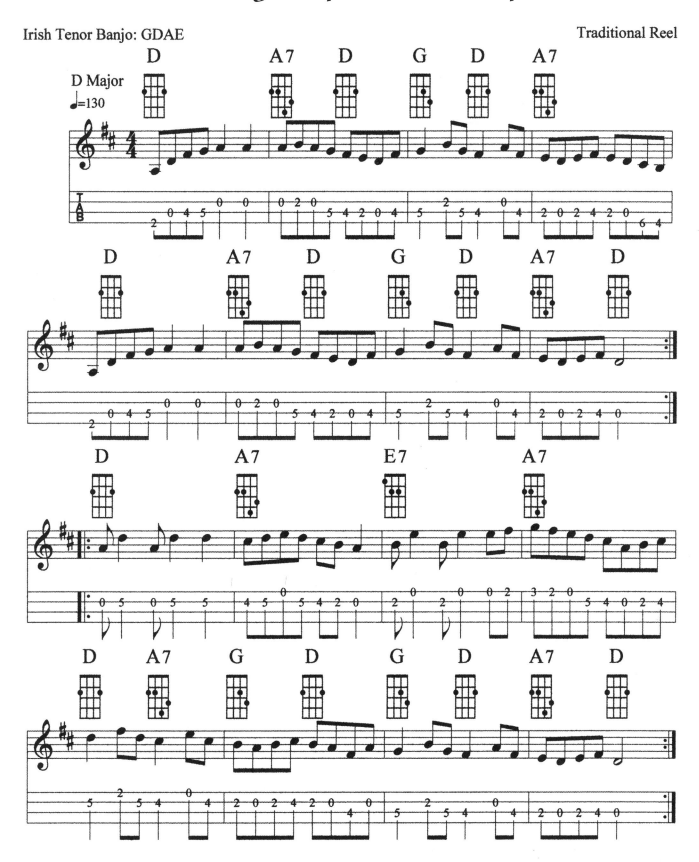

Wind that Shakes the Barley

Irish Tenor Banjo; GDAE

Traditional Jig

More Great Books from Dick Sheridan...

More Great Banjo Books from Centerstream...

BEGINNING CLAWHAMMER BANJO
DVD
by Ken Perlman

Ken Perlman is one of the most celebrated clawhammer banjo stylists performing today. In this new DVD, he teaches how to play this exciting style, with ample close-ups and clear explanations of techniques such as: hand positions, chords, tunings, brush-thumb, single-string strokes, hammer-ons, pull-offs and slides. Songs include: Boatsman • Cripple Creek • Pretty Polly. Includes a transcription booklet. 60 minutes.
00000330 DVD $19.95

INTERMEDIATE CLAWHAMMER BANJO
DVD
by Ken Perlman

Picking up where *Beginning Clawhammer Banjo* leaves off, this DVD begins with a review of brush thumbing and the single-string stroke, then moves into specialized techniques such as: drop- and double-thumbing, single-string brush thumb, chords in double "C" tuning, and more. Tunes include: Country Waltz • Green Willis • Little Billie Wilson • Magpie • The Meeting of the Waters • Old Joe Clark • and more! Includes a transcription booklet. 60 minutes.
00000331 DVD $19.95

CLAWHAMMER STYLE BANJO
TAB DVD
A Complete Guide for Beginning and Advanced Banjo Players
by Ken Perlman

This handbook covers basic right & left-hand positions, simple chords, and fundamental clawhammer techniques: the brush, the "bumm-titty" strum, pull-offs, and slides. There is also instruction on more complicated picking, double thumbing, quick slides, fretted pull-offs, harmonics, improvisation, and more. Includes over 40 fun-to-play banjo tunes.
00000118 Book Only.. $19.95
00000334 DVD $39.95

THE EARLY MINSTREL BANJO
TAB
by Joe Weidlich

Featuring more than 65 classic songs, this interesting book teaches how to play the minstrel banjo like players who were part of various popular troupes in 1865. The book includes: a short history of the banjo, including the origins of the minstrel show; info on the construction of minstrel banjos, chapters on each of the seven major banjo methods published through the end of the Civil War; songs from each method in banjo tablature, many available for the first time; info on how to arrange songs for the minstrel banjo; a reference list of contemporary gut and nylon string gauges approximating historical banjo string tensions in common usage during the antebellum period (for those Civil War re-enactors who wish to achieve that old-time "minstrel banjo" sound); an extensive cross-reference list of minstrel banjo song titles found in the major antebellum banjo methods; and more. (266 pages)
00000325... $29.95

MELODIC CLAWHAMMER BANJO

A Comprehensive Guide to Modern Clawhammer Banjo
by Ken Perlman

Ken Perlman, today's foremost player of the style, brings you this comprehensive guide to the melodic clawhammer. Over 50 tunes in clear tablature. Learn to play authentic versions of Appalachian fiddle tunes, string band tunes, New England hornpipes, Irish jigs, Scottish reels, and more. Includes arrangements by many important contemporary players, and chapters on basic and advanced techniques. Also features over 70 musical illustrations, plus historical notes, and period photos.
00000412 Book/CD Pack $19.95

MINSTREL BANJO – BRIGGS' BANJO INSTRUCTOR
INCLUDES TAB
by Joseph Weidlich

The Banjo Instructor by Tom Briggs, published in 1855, was the first complete method for banjo. It contained "many choice plantation melodies," "a rare collection of quaint old dances," and the "elementary principles of music." This edition is a reprinting of the original Briggs' *Banjo Instructor*, made up-to-date with modern explanations, tablature, and performance notes. It teaches how to hold the banjo, movements, chords, slurs and more, and includes 68 banjo solo songs that Briggs presumably learned directly from slaves.
00000221... $12.95

MORE MINSTREL BANJO
INCLUDES TAB
by Joseph Weidlich

This is the second book in a 3-part series of intabulations of music for the minstrel (Civil War-era) banjo. Adapted from Frank Converse's *Banjo Instructor, Without a Master* (published in New York in 1865), this book contains a choice collection of banjo solos, jigs, songs, reels, walk arounds, and more, progressively arranged and plainly explained, enabling players to become proficient banjoists. Thorough measure-by-measure explanations are provided for each of the songs, all of which are part of the traditional minstrel repertoire.
00000258... $12.95

WITH MY BANJO ON MY KNEE

The Minstrel Songs of Stephen Foster
arr. for banjo by Daniel Partner
Historical notes by Edwin J. Sims

Here are some of the first and most popular songs ever written for banjo. Fascinating historical notes accompany this collection, describing the meaning of the songs, their place in history, the significance of the musicians who first performed them, and Foster himself, America's first professional songwriter. The complete original lyrics of each song and an extensive bibliography are included. The CD contains recordings of each arrangement performed on solo minstrel banjo.
00001179 Book/CD Pack $19.95

CENTERSTREAM®

P.O. Box 17878 - Anaheim Hills, CA 92817
(714) 779-9390   www.centerstream-usa.com